THE GILDE

A History from Beginning to End

Copyright © 2019 by Hourly History.

Table of Contents

Introduction

In 1872, writer Samuel Langhorne Clemens, better known to most people by his literary pseudonym Mark Twain, was at a dinner party where he began chatting to his neighbor, friend, and fellow novelist, Charles Dudley Warner. The two men began to discuss what they saw as the decline in standards in the United States since the Civil War. Materialism and greed seemed rampant, they agreed, politics was corrupt, and a few people were becoming extremely rich by exploiting thousands who were forced to live in poverty and work in appalling conditions. The two writers decided to collaborate on a novel which would satirize the current state of America.

The Gilded Age: A Tale of Today was published in 1873. It never became as popular as Mark Twain's later works which included *The Adventures of Tom Sawyer* and *The Adventures of Huckleberry Finn*, but it did have the distinction of providing a name for a particular period of American history—events in the United States from 1870 to 1900 are now generally known as the Gilded Age. The name was chosen by Twain to draw a contrast with a Golden Age. In a Golden Age, Twain contended, life is good for everyone. But in a Gilded Age, there is only a thin surface of gold over underlying base metal, a metaphor for a small number of fabulously wealthy people who grew rich by exploiting vast numbers who lived in poverty. The title of the book found resonance with many people and, even while it was still in progress, this period became widely known as the Gilded Age.

The last quarter of the nineteenth century was a time of enormous change. Reconstruction after the Civil War produced fundamental changes to the American way of life. Technological advancements, including the extension of the railroad system, changed people's relationship with the very landscape of America. An industrial revolution brought affordable products for many and great wealth for a few. Conspicuous consumption became truly conspicuous for the first time while poverty remained widespread for the majority of the population. New waves of immigrants changed the very nature of American society.

In just thirty years, the United States went from the Wild West to the Wright Brothers testing their first flying machine, from being a mainly agrarian nation to one of the world's leading industrial powers. This is the story of the Gilded Age of America.

Chapter One

Legacy of the Civil War

"America has no north, no south, no east, no west. The sun rises over the hills and sets over the mountains, the compass just points up and down, and we can laugh now at the absurd notion of there being a north and a south. We are one and undivided."

—Sam Watkins, on the end of the Civil War

The American Civil War between the secessionist Confederate States of the south and the Unionist States of the north raged from 1861 to 1865. When it was over, the United States was restored, though the country itself was far from united. Three-quarters of a million people died during the conflict and many cities were damaged. In the south, roads, railroads, and industrial capacity were virtually destroyed, and an economy which was had been based on the availability of slave labor was no longer viable. Many cities were damaged or even razed, and starvation and disease stalked the country, especially affecting newly emancipated slaves who had few resources to call upon.

The period following the end of the Civil War has become known as the Reconstruction Era and this period overlaps the Gilded Age. From 1865 to the middle of the 1870s, reconstruction followed two distinct strands: The political integration of the southern states into the Union and the rebuilding of infrastructure and industry in the south.

Immediately following the end of the war, the north established military administrations in many southern states until new governments which accepted the constitution of the Union, and particularly the 14th Amendment which gave freed slaves the right to vote, could be formed. Up to 15,000 former Confederate officers were temporarily barred from voting and numbers of northerners, contemptuously called "carpetbaggers" by many southerners, moved into the southern states accompanied by educated blacks from the north. These people helped to set up the first elected assemblies in the south, which were required to swear allegiance to the Union before they could take over power from the military authorities. By 1869, all eleven southern states had elected bodies in place, though the disenfranchised former Confederate officers wouldn't be given the vote until 1872.

The rebuilding of the infrastructure and cities of the south progressed even as political assemblies were being created. The expansion of the southern railroad system in particular was seen as an important element in restoring industry and ending isolation, and many millions of dollars in subsidies were offered for this purpose. Many southern farms and plantations which had relied on slave labor were no longer viable after the end of the war, and a process known as sharecropping became popular.

Sharecropping involved a landowner leasing out part of their land and providing housing, tools, and seeds to a farmer who was also expected to obtain food and supplies on credit from local merchants. At harvest time, the cropper kept a proportion of the crop (generally from one-third to one-half) while the remainder went to the landowner. The cropper was also expected to pay the merchant from their share. However, in bad years, the cropper's share often wasn't sufficient to pay off their debt to the merchant, and this was then carried through to the next year. This left croppers, who were initially mainly black but later also white, extremely poor and often in so much debt that they could never make any money for themselves.

The situation in the north was quite different. American industrial capacity had always been centered in the northeast—more than 80% of U.S. manufacturing capacity was based in northern states, and at the outbreak of the Civil War, New York and Pennsylvania each had more industrial capacity than all the southern states combined. The population of the north was mainly concentrated in urban centers with farmers in the west providing food. During the war, the need to produce weapons and supplies for the military had encouraged even more industrialization in the northern states, and this continued after the war ended.

In the years following the end of the Civil War, the south remained mainly agrarian with many people, including emancipated slaves, living in abject poverty under the sharecropping system. In the north, the drive towards industrialization continued. However, the main focus of interest for many Americans following the Civil War was neither the south nor the north, but rather the untamed wilderness of the west.

Chapter Two

Taming the Wild West

"Go West, young man!"

—Horace Greeley, 1865

In the 1870s, America was divided not just into northern and southern states, but into the east and the west. In the east were states that had previously comprised the Confederacy and the Union. To the west were just three states: California, Nevada, and Oregon. In between was a vast area of unincorporated and largely unsettled territories. In 1862, the Homestead Act was passed specifically to encourage migration to the west. Any American citizen could travel to the west and settle on a surveyed 160-acre lot. Provided that they remained there for a minimum of five years and built a home, they could then claim the land as their own. The intention was to encourage settlers to develop the vast, empty areas of the west. The problem was that these areas weren't actually empty—they were occupied by a large number of Native American tribes whose treatment by the U.S. government forms one of the most shameful episodes of American history.

In the early 1800s, the United States adopted the Monroe Doctrine, a policy based on lofty ideals which stated that America would not tolerate the exploitation of native people in America by European powers. In practice, this simply meant that these people would instead be exploited by Americans. It is interesting to note that, in a period when there were widespread debate about the emancipation of black people and the rights of African-Americans, almost no-one seems to have objected to the virtual extermination of Native American tribes. The first president of the United States, George Washington, a man generally considered enlightened and liberal, said of Native Americans: "Indians and wolves are both beasts of prey, tho' they differ in shape." One hundred years later, there is little evidence that this attitude had fundamentally changed.

The Indian Removal Act of 1830 gave the government the right to forcibly remove Native Americans from virtually any area they chose. The brutal removal of Native America tribes from states such as Georgia led one chief to call this act "a trail of tears and death" for his people. By the beginning of the Gilded Age, Native Americans had been almost completely removed from the eastern states. However, in the west, many still lived in their tribal homelands, and a conflict with the new waves of settlers encouraged by the Homestead Act was inevitable.

The movement of settlers was intensified in 1869 by the completion of the first transcontinental railroad which connected the existing railroad network in the east with San Francisco on the west coast. No longer would settlers be forced to spend weeks or months on arduous and dangerous wagon trails—now they could travel between New York and San Francisco by railroad in just six days.

In 1872, in eastern California, conflict erupted between the U.S. military and the Modoc people. The outcome was that the remaining men, women, and children of the Modoc tribe were transported to Indian Territory in Oklahoma where they remained as prisoners of war until 1909. The Great Sioux War of 1876 included the massacre of General George Custer and his men at the Battle of Little Bighorn, but ended in the defeat of the Lakota tribe, the appropriation of their lands, and the remainder of the tribe were forced on to reservations. Another conflict began in 1877 when members of the Nez Perce were forced to move from their ancestral lands on the Pacific Northwest, despite the fact that the U.S. government had signed a treaty promising them this land in perpetuity in 1855. After a number of battles with the U.S. military, the Nez Perce tribe was defeated and forced on to a reservation in 1878.

Faced with organized troops using the most advanced weapons of the day, the Native Americans stood little chance. Virtually the last large-scale encounter between the U.S. military and Native Americans occurred at Wounded Knee Creek in South Dakota in 1890. U.S. cavalry supported by Hotchkiss mountain guns surrounded a camp of the Lakota tribe and were in the process of disarming the men when shooting began. Between 150 to 300 Lakota men, women, and children were massacred. Twenty American soldiers were awarded the Medal of Honor for their part in this action which marked the end of large-scale armed Native American resistance to expansion in the west.

However, though the Native American threat may have been reduced, the west was still wild. During the 1870s, the legend of the cowboy and the gunman began to emerge (though they were also variously known as shootists or pistoleers at the time). Newspapers, pamphlets, and books strained to satisfy a seemingly insatiable desire for information about colorful characters including "Wild Bill" Hickok, "Buffalo Bill" Cody, "Calamity Jane" Canary, William "Billy the Kid" Bonney, and Jesse James. For readers living in the relative calm of the east, the adventures of criminals and lawmen began a fascination with the Wild West that has never abated. Events such as the gunfight at the O.K. Corral in Tombstone in 1881 and the death of Jesse James in 1882 made headlines even in eastern newspapers. When William Cody brought his *Buffalo Bill's Wild West* traveling show to the eastern states in 1883, he sold millions of tickets. For the most part, stories about the west were exaggerated (or sometimes invented completely) by journalists and writers who wanted to sell copy. Ideas such as the Code of the West and even the notion of gunfights being a common or even an honorable way to settle a dispute had little basis in reality, but these things have passed into American folklore.

Part of the reason for this fascination was that life in the east was changing dramatically. America was becoming an industrialized nation and nostalgia was increasing for what was seen as a simpler way of life in the west. While settlers in the west were concerned about the day-to-day realities of surviving in a harsh environment, people in the east wanted to escape from the poverty and drudgery of their lives by reading about frontier adventure and excitement.

Chapter Three

The Rise of Industrialization

"A land that had once run largely north-south now ran east-west. Each change could have been traced back to the railroads."

—Richard White, *Railroaded*

The Second Industrial Revolution, the transition from a traditional farming-based economy to a modern industrialized nation, took place in America during the Gilded Age. A major factor in this transformation was the expansion of the railroad network. Even before 1870, the U.S. railroad network was well established, especially in what had been the Union States during the Civil War. By 1869, the first transcontinental railroad had been completed linking this eastern network with the city of San Francisco on the west coast. However, after 1870, railroad expansion continued at an even more rapid pace than before.

By 1880, the railroad industry was America's largest employer apart from farming, and the network operated 22,000 passenger locomotives and 18,000 freight locomotives. During the 1880s, 75,000 miles of new railroad track was added to the U.S. network, the largest accumulation of new lines anywhere in the world. In 1860, railroads had moved half as much freight as inland waterways such as the mighty Mississippi River; by 1890, railroads were moving five times more freight than all inland waterways combined. This massive expansion of railroads made possible huge changes in agriculture and industry.

For the first time, produce from the interior of the country could be shipped rapidly to the growing cities in the east. Communities which had previously been completely isolated were suddenly accessible. Goods manufactured in the east could be distributed across the whole country. This brought about massive changes, not just in American society, but in the landscape itself. Vast areas of grassland were replaced with fields of corn and wheat. Plains, where once mighty herds of bison had roamed, were replaced with grazing for cattle. The Native American tribes who had relied on the bison for food and clothing were confined to reservations. Towns and cities were established and grew in areas where once there had been virtually no inhabitants. Railroads were generally also accompanied by telegraph lines, allowing almost instant communication over the vast regions of the American interior. The railroad network also meant that local communities were no longer totally reliant on the success or failure of crops in their immediate area. Because most communities were now connected to the rail infrastructure, the failure of one crop no longer meant the possibility of starvation for people in the immediate area.

The federal government, recognizing the importance of railroads in the transformation of America, assisted the private companies who built the new networks. Land was granted to railroad companies to encourage expansion and new construction. The price of coal was maintained at a low level to allow steam locomotives to be run at a reasonable cost. Where the homelands of Native American tribes stood in the way of new railroad lines, the government used the U.S. Army to clear them away. It seemed that nothing could halt the growth of the railroads, and the word "railroaded" entered the vocabulary of the nation, meaning coercing or forcing someone to do something against their will.

In conjunction with the rise of railroads, the U.S. steel industry also developed rapidly in the Gilded Age. New techniques for producing steel meant that this material could be produced cheaply, and steel was used to build bridges and rails as well as allowing new methods of construction for buildings.

Railroads also allowed the movement of heavy equipment to remote areas, promoting the increasing mechanization of farming. By 1870, steam engines did more work on American farms than humans and animals combined, and mechanical reapers were becoming more common. By the 1890s, the availability of tractors powered by internal combustion engines did even more work that had previously been done by men and horses. This meant that farms needed fewer workers which contributed to a massive migration from rural areas to cities, especially the cities of the east. During the Gilded Age, millions of American moved from rural areas to cities.

The prospect that drew people to cities was the widespread availability of unskilled work. Manufacturing was increasingly being done in large factories made possible by improvements in building techniques and the ready availability of water and gas supplies and sewage facilities. The railroad network made it possible to bring raw material to factories and to distribute goods outside the local area, making it possible for factories to produce items in very large quantities, which in turn also made it possible to keep prices down. This, combined with increasing mechanization of the manufacturing process, led to a high demand for unskilled and semi-skilled workers.

It was a fundamental change—previously, people had produced a single product in a workshop, being involved in every stage of the process. Now, workers performed a single repetitive task in a mill or factory, day after day. This change from the use of artisans to unskilled workers who were not required to understand the nature of what they did changed the face of employment in the United States. Skilled workers were replaced by unskilled, and many women, children, and immigrants were employed at lower rates to perform tasks that had previously been the work of skilled craftsmen. The use of children in the workplace meant that large numbers did not go to school—families needed income from every family member, and it often wasn't possible for children to attend school at all.

The widespread need for unskilled labor combined with the availability of products at lower prices led to a notable improvement in American living standards and, with 14 million new immigrants arriving in the United States during the Gilded Age, there was no shortage of potential workers. However, life for these workers was far from easy—working conditions were often poor, there were no healthcare or pension provisions, and work itself was dangerous. Workers were commonly required to work for 12 hours or more without substantial breaks, and they were often working with steam engines and potentially dangerous machinery. Fatigue, heat, and fumes all contributed to making workers more liable to make mistakes—in the years 1880 to 1900, an average of 35,000 workers died every year in mine and factory accidents. It was the highest mortality rate for workers in the developed world at the time, and it means that, during the Gilded Age, more people died in workplace accidents than were killed in the whole of the American Civil War.

There was also very little job security for workers. Employees could be dismissed with little notice, and employers were keen to increase profits by hiring workers at the lowest possible cost. Increasing mechanization meant that some unskilled jobs could be replaced by machines leading to a loss of employment.

Industrialization was therefore both a positive and a negative influence for the vast majority of Americans. It provided employment for very large numbers of people and it made goods available at low cost, but workers were left without job security and often worked in difficult, exhausting, and frequently dangerous conditions. However, for a small number of Americans, the Second Industrial Revolution brought wealth on an almost unimaginable scale.

Chapter Four

Robber Barons and Captains of Industry

"Take not from the mouth of labor the bread it has earned."

—Thomas Jefferson

During the Gilded Age, a small number of industrialists became incredibly wealthy and powerful. Some people viewed these people as Captains of Industry, entrepreneurs of vision and daring whose business acumen provided work for thousands of people. However, for others, the unscrupulous actions of these men called to mind the ruthless Robber Barons of the medieval period who used their power to suppress the lower classes and to accumulate vast wealth while ignoring poverty. In truth, many of these successful and wealthy men combined elements of both.

John D. Rockefeller was born in 1839 into a large and not particularly wealthy family in upstate New York. When he was 16, Rockefeller got a job as a bookkeeper, and it soon became evident that this young man had an affinity for business. In the 1860s, Rockefeller was involved in several companies which refined oil, and in 1870, he began what would be his most successful operation when he co-founded Standard Oil with several partners. Standard Oil quickly established a virtual monopoly on the supply of kerosene and gasoline in the U.S. just at a time when this product was becoming vitally important.

Kerosene and gasoline were widely used for lighting at the beginning of the Gilded Age, and other products of oil refining were used as lubricants for machines. As electricity became more widely available, the use of oil-based products for domestic lighting declined but, fortunately for Rockefeller and Standard Oil, just as this was happening, the use of the internal combustion engine was becoming more common, and this required gasoline as fuel. Standard Oil generated considerable wealth for its owners, and Rockefeller also became an influential part-owner of many of the railroad businesses which he used to transport oil products across America.

There is no doubt that Rockefeller was a skilled and ruthless businessman. He drove a number of competitors out of business without any qualms—he once said "competition is a sin," and there were no regulations preventing the creation of monopolies during the Gilded Age. Rockefeller was also ready to buy the support of politicians when this suited his purpose, and politics during the Gilded Age was almost completely dominated by corruption and graft. However, Rockefeller was extremely religious, was never heard to swear, didn't smoke or drink, and for entertainment in the evenings, he and his family would sing hymns together. In his personal life, Rockefeller was frugal—he enjoyed playing golf, for example, but always used old golf balls in case they should get lost. When he saw other players using new balls, he once exclaimed "they must be rich!"

The truth was that John D. Rockefeller was very rich indeed. Some people claim that he was the richest American there has ever been—certainly he was the wealthiest man of Gilded Age. Rockefeller was the first American billionaire, and his fortune was estimated to be worth around 2% of the U.S. national economy. When his friend J. P. Morgan died in 1913 and left a fortune worth $80 million, Rockefeller supposedly exclaimed in surprise, "And to think he wasn't even a rich man!"

However, although the accusation that he was the archetype of the Robber Baron was often made about Rockefeller, he was also well known for the sheer amount of money that he gave away. Even when he was just sixteen and working for a comparatively low wage, Rockefeller made sure that he gave at least six percent of his earnings to those less fortunate than himself. As he became wealthier, the scale of his philanthropy also grew. In 1884, Rockefeller provided money to found the Atlanta Baptist Female Seminary in Atlanta, a college for African-American women. He gave $80 million to the University of Chicago, allowing it to grow into a world-class institution by the end of the century. By the 1880s, Rockefeller was receiving thousands of letters each month asking for money. It became his habit to gather his family each morning after breakfast to review these appeals for help and to decide which should receive money.

Rockefeller retired from business just after the beginning of the twentieth century, though he continued to set up charitable foundations and research organizations until the end of his life in 1937. His rise to power and accumulation of wealth coincided completely with the Gilded Age, and during this period he amassed a personal fortune that dwarfs almost any other (as a percentage of the United States GDP, not even Bill Gates or Jeff Bezos would come close to Rockefeller's fortune). However, he also gave away staggering sums, and there is good reason to refer to Rockefeller as the greatest philanthropist there has ever been.

The only person who came close to rivaling the personal wealth of John D. Rockefeller during the Gilded Age was a Scottish immigrant named Andrew Carnegie. Carnegie was born in Dunfermline, Scotland in 1835 and moved to the

United States in 1848 when his parents emigrated. One of Carnegie's first jobs was as a telegraph messenger boy for the Ohio Telegraph Company, and during the next 15 years, he worked for railroads and telegraph companies. He began to accumulate serious wealth when he founded the Keystone Bridge Company, a steel mill which soon began producing steel for railroads and to make weapons and other items for the Union States during the Civil War.

By 1890, Carnegie controlled the bulk of the American steel industry just at the point that the production of steel in the U.S. finally surpassed production in Britain, formerly the most prolific steel producer. Like Rockefeller, Carnegie amassed a staggering personal fortune. However, also like Rockefeller, Carnegie saw no benefit in simply accumulating wealth, and he too gave away vast sums. In the 1880s, he wrote: "Man must have no idol and the amassing of wealth is one of the worst species of idolatry! No idol is more debasing than the worship of money!" At the same time, Carnegie decided that he would personally take no more than $50,000 out of his business each year—the rest he would give away. Considering that in some years he made more than $20 million, that amounted to a very great deal of money indeed.

In 1889, Carnegie wrote an extremely influential article, *The Gospel of Wealth*, which was published in the *North American Review* magazine. He argued that there should be two parts to any wealthy person's life: the first involved the accumulation of wealth, the second its distribution to those in need. During his life, it is estimated that Carnegie gave away donations worth more than $75 billion in today's figures. Many of these donations were used to fund research and educational institutes in the United States and in his native Scotland. When he died in 1919, the remainder of Carnegie's fortune was given to foundations and charities.

John Pierpont Morgan was born in 1837 as a son of an influential banking family in Hartford, Connecticut. Morgan came to dominate banking during the Gilded Age and became one of the most powerful men of the period. He entered the New York banking world in the 1850s, and by 1871, he was so well respected that he formed his own bank, J.P. Morgan & Co. Morgan worked with some of the most significant entrepreneurs of the Gilded Age and some of the biggest corporations, and he is credited with virtually inventing what would now be called corporate banking.

Morgan specialized in mergers and acquisitions: he was directly responsible for the consolidation of several companies owned by Thomas Edison to form Edison General Electric. He was also responsible for the 1892 merger between that company and the Thomson-Houston Electric Company to form General Electric, one of the largest corporations in America and one of the original 12 companies listed on the Dow Jones Industrial Average when it was formed in 1896. Morgan was also involved in a series of deals which allowed the Bell Telephone Company to evolve into the American Telephone and Telegraph Company (later to re-brand as AT&T) in 1885.

During the Gilded Age, J.P. Morgan & Co. were involved in financing or underwriting securities for many of the major American corporations including International Harvester, the United States Steel Corporation, and most of the larger railroads. John P. Morgan was also directly involved in the evolution of corporate finance in America. When J.P. Morgan & Co. was founded, Wall Street was simply one of several centers competing to be the heart of American finance. With his assistance, it became a unified group of businesses which were responsible for financing what had become the most important industrial power on the planet. Not everyone appreciated Morgan's style—he could be ruthless, and he never forgot an insult, real or imagined.

However, not even his detractors could deny how much he shaped corporate finance during the emergence of American industrial power—never before or since has one man had so much influence over the financial institutions of a large nation.

Morgan also invested heavily in many of the companies which he helped consolidate, and he was able to amass a considerable personal fortune. His wealth may have appeared insignificant to a multi-millionaire like John D. Rockefeller, but to most people in America, J. P. Morgan was very rich indeed. Morgan also donated a large proportion of his wealth to charities, hospitals, schools, and churches, and when he died in 1913, his vast and valuable art collection was donated to the Metropolitan Museum of Art in New York City.

The Second Industrial Revolution heralded great change in America which in turn allowed the creation of new corporations and, with the assistance of forward-looking bankers such as J. P. Morgan, these large companies provided enormous wealth for their founders and owners as well as employment for a significant proportion of the U.S. population. These wealthy people were few, but their fabulous wealth, lavish lifestyles, houses, cars, and other possessions formed the gilding on the Gilded Age. Often people like John D. Rockefeller and Andrew Carnegie are seen as typifying this era. However, life for the vast majority of ordinary Americans during the Gilded Age was very different indeed.

Chapter Five

Poverty and Inequality

*"If the United States, like the countries of the Old World,
are also to grow vast crops of poor, desperate, dissatisfied,
nomadic, miserably-waged populations such as we see
looming upon us of late years—steadily, even if slowly,
eating into us like a cancer of lungs or stomach—then our
republican experiment, notwithstanding all its surface
successes, is at heart an unhealthy failure."*

—Walt Whitman

The emergence of giant corporations in the United States
during the Gilded Age provided employment for millions of
Americans. It was, however, a very different type of
employment to what had been before. Up to the Civil War,
the majority of Americans worked on the land in some way,
either as farmers or ranchers or as subsistence farmers
supplementing their income in other ways. Those who
produced goods or provided specific services were generally
skilled people who had learned a particular craft over a long
period. As the Gilded Age began in the 1870s, this was
changing dramatically.

Modern industrialization requires ready access to raw
materials and distribution channels for manufactured goods.
Large and mechanized factories required access to a nearby
labor force which meant that they had to be established close
to urban areas. The modernized manufacturing processes
required large numbers of unskilled workers, and the
cheapest source of this labor was often women and children.
With the increasing mechanization of farming, there wasn't

as much need for agricultural workers as there previously had been, and people began to gravitate towards cities because that was where they could find work.

Most cities, however, weren't prepared for this influx of new residents. Water supplies were inadequate, and garbage and sewage soon accumulated in the streets. Where there were sewage pipes, these dumped raw waste into rivers which were often also the main source of drinking water. Many workers, especially the large numbers of new immigrants, lived in tenement housing. Tenement buildings were constructed close together and had no garden or yard. The buildings were up to six stories tall with four three-room apartments per floor. Often, the only rooms which had windows were those that faced the front. In 1879, new building regulations were passed which required that all rooms in tenements must have access to air from outside. To ensure that this didn't interfere with the ability to cram as many tenants into a space as possible, a new type of tenement was produced: the dumbbell tenement. These apartments incorporated a narrow air shaft in the center of the building. However, the shafts soon proved hazardous as they rapidly became blocked with garbage and allowed fires to spread more easily from apartment to apartment.

Many eastern U.S. cities developed large areas of overcrowded tenement housing during the Gilded Age. In New York City, for example, by 1900 there were over 80,000 tenements (mainly on the Lower East Side) housing over two million residents. In most cities, the collection of garbage was not organized, and in many places rotting garbage lay in the streets mixing with effluent from overflowing cesspools. In the summer, the stench was unbelievable, and disease was a major problem. Cholera and yellow fever epidemics regularly swept through areas of poor housing, and tuberculosis caused large numbers of deaths. A cholera outbreak in Birmingham, Alabama in 1873 killed 128 people. Due to disease and other factors, over 25% of children born in American cities during the Gilded Age failed to survive past their first birthday. Major improvements in tenement housing would not begin until the passing of the Tenement House Act in 1901.

Of course, even paying the rent on an apartment in an overcrowded tenement building cost money. Fortunately, there were lots of factories in urban areas which provided employment for large numbers of unskilled workers. Unfortunately, this work was badly paid and insecure. Working environments were often dangerous, overheated, and exposed workers to toxic substances. Employment contracts could be arbitrarily ended, there was no sick pay or paid vacation, and if a worker became injured or too ill to work, they were simply dismissed. Work was also exhausting—workers were often required to labor for twelve hours per day, six days per week. Some employers, like steel mills, demanded a seven-day work week. Exhaustion combined with dangerous working conditions took a toll on workers. In 1882, an average of 675 workers died each week in workplace accidents—and this number does not include workers injured so badly that they could not continue to work.

Wages were generally low to the extent that it was necessary for every member of the family to work just to bring in enough money for rent and food. By 1890, four million women were working for wages in the United States (this does not include the large numbers of women, such as seamstresses, who undertook piecework at home) and this number would double within twenty years. Twenty percent of boys under fifteen years of age were in full-time employment, and children as young as five were employed in factories and mills. Children were popular as employees because they cost relatively little.

In 1889, children were being paid around 27 cents for a 12-hour shift. Of course, working meant that children could not attend school, and many were forced to abandon any hope of improving their position in order to help their families meet their day-to-day needs. Women were also popular as employees because they were paid around half the wage for men—women received an average of 267 dollars per year in 1889 for working ten hours each day, six days a week. In the same year, Andrew Carnegie made 23 million dollars, on which he was not required to pay any income tax.

Unsurprisingly, crime increased dramatically in areas of poor housing in the Gilded Age. The people who lived there were paid so little that they were unable to accumulate savings—any interruption to work for any reason meant that the whole family went hungry. Crime offered an alternative means of putting food on the table. The incidence of theft, assault, burglary, and murder in major U.S. cities rose sharply during this period. So too did the amount spent on policing, though in many cities police spent the majority of their time and resources protecting the more affluent areas while those living in tenement ghettos were virtually left to fend for themselves.

Alcoholism was also a growing issue as was the use of narcotics as both provided a temporary escape from the unpleasant realities of working-class life. Drugs such as cocaine and cannabis were still legal and widely included in various tonics and other preparations said to promote good health. Other narcotics such as opium, laudanum, and morphine were also freely available. Alcohol was widely available, relatively inexpensive, and uncontrolled advertising was able to promote beer and spirits as healthy and restorative.

The Gilded Age also saw the rise of gang culture. Young men in working-class neighborhoods with nothing to look forward to other than a life of exhausting and underpaid work sought other routes to money, prestige, and power. These criminal gangs were often organized on an ethnic basis, with immigrants of Irish, Italian, and Chinese extraction being particularly prevalent. In areas of some U.S. cities, gangs became so powerful that they effectively controlled the streets. For example, in the 1890s a particularly brutal gang called the Gophers effectively ruled the West Side of New York City between Ninth and Eleventh Avenues and either side of Forty-Second Street. The Gophers fought regularly with their rivals, the Hudson Dusters, causing many deaths. They also extorted money from local businesses and provided a basis for the organized crime gangs that emerged in the twentieth century.

The contrast between the lives of the few very wealthy people during this period and the squalor in which many members of the working class lived is especially striking. Conditions for low-income families were often truly desperate, and it was directly through their exploitation that the rich grew even richer. In these circumstances, the struggle of workers to organize themselves and to improve their working conditions became a major feature of this period.

Chapter Six

Emergence of Labor Unions and Women's Movements

"We mean to uphold the dignity of labor."

—Part of the initiation oath for the Knights of Labor

Given the substandard working conditions which faced most working-class people, it is logical that the Gilded Age also saw the rise of popular labor movements in the United States. The first large labor union in the U.S. was the National Labor Union, founded in 1866. The NLU attempted to engage in collective bargaining with business owners to increase wages and improve working conditions. However, the NLU was hampered because the large numbers of immigrants and the influx of people to cities meant that employers could afford to dismiss workers who threatened to strike and replace them with others who were not affiliated with a union. The NLU was further impeded because it did not allow women or black people to join. The NLU lasted just six years, and during the Panic of 1873, it effectively ceased to exist.

The Knights of Labor began as a secret workers' society in 1869, but it became a labor union after the failure of the NLU. Unlike the NLU, the Knights of Labor allowed membership for both women and black people, and in the 1870s and 1880s it was successful in organizing strikes that led to some improvement in wages and conditions for workers, though just like the NLU it was hampered by the widespread availability of non-union labor. By the mid-1880s, the Knights of Labor had over 700,000 members.

The reaction of employers to strikes during the Gilded Age was often violent and sometimes brutal. In May 1886, at a gathering of workers involved in a strike organized by the Knights of Labor in Chicago, police opened fire and killed several strikers. At a demonstration the following day at Haymarket Square in Chicago, someone threw a bomb as police advanced to disperse demonstrators. Seven police officers and four protestors were killed in the bomb blast and an ensuing exchange of gunfire. Several members of an anarchist group were arrested and accused of the bombing, and the Knights of Labor were also (falsely) accused of involvement. The following year, the Knights of Labor organized a strike of sugar cane workers in Louisiana. As a result of the strike, many black workers and their families were evicted from their homes, and a large number sought refuge in the town of Thibodaux. While there, the strikers were attacked by white militia groups and up to 50 black men, women, and children were killed. The strikers returned to work without achieving any of their demands, and as a result of this and other perceived failures, the Knights of Labor declined in popularity.

However, as the Knights of Labor were in decline, another labor group, the American Federation of Labor, was growing in popularity. The AFL acted as coordinator for a number of smaller independent unions, though it represented only white, male, skilled workers. Like the labor unions which had come before, the AFL campaigned for shorter working hours, better wages, and improved working conditions. However, its efforts were impeded by continuing violent reactions to strikes.

In July 1892, a strike was organized by the Amalgamated Association of Iron and Steel Workers and the Knights of

Labor at a steel plant operated by Andrew Carnegie's Carnegie Steel Company in Homestead, Pennsylvania. The steel company hired armed members of the Pinkerton Detective Agency to seize the plant from striking workers, and during a twelve-hour gun battle, at least three Pinkerton agents and seven strikers were shot dead and many more were injured. Finally, 8,000 soldiers of the Pennsylvania militia were called in to evict the strikers from the plant. The Carnegie Steel Company then hired replacement non-union workers and the plant continued in operation. Many of the strikers were forced to re-apply for their own jobs, often at reduced wages.

Like many of the strikes organized during the Gilded Age, the Homestead strike was brutally repressed and resulted in a complete defeat for the labor unions. Yet the AFL survived and went on to become one of the most powerful labor unions in the United States. Although the AFL, like many other organizations in the U.S. during this period, was only open to men, the Gilded Age also saw the beginning of several influential women's movements.

In 1869, two important women's groups were created in America: The American Women's Suffrage Association (AWSA) was founded by Lucy Stone and Julia Ward Howe in the Boston area with the intention of campaigning for female suffrage on a state-by-state basis. Meanwhile the National Women's Suffrage Association was formed by Susan B. Anthony and Elizabeth Cady Stanton in New York with the aim of changing the Constitution and giving all American women the right to vote. After years of intense rivalry, the two groups combined in 1890 to become the National American Woman Suffrage Association under the leadership of Susan Anthony.

This group became very successful in lobbying politicians and in attracting attention through marches, demonstrations, and other acts. By 1896, four states,

Wyoming, Colorado, Utah, and Idaho, had granted women the right to vote. And it wasn't just in the realm of suffrage that women's groups became important during the Gilded Age. In 1874, a social reform group called the Women's Christian Temperance Union (WCTU) was created. This group aimed to produce a "sober and pure world" by promoting purity, evangelical Christianity, and abstinence from alcohol and tobacco. By the end of the Gilded Age, the WCTU had become the largest women's movement in the world with more than 150,000 active members in the United States alone. This group wasn't just concerned with temperance—under the charismatic leadership of its second president, Frances Willard, it also promoted women's rights and lobbied for increased opportunities for women.

Many people in America were suspicious of both labor unions and women's groups, seeing these organizations as responsible for undermining the country's prosperity. However, there was another threat that was much more concerning and that was a new wave of immigration which reached the United States during the Gilded Age.

Chapter Seven

The New Immigrants

"The happy and powerful do not go into exile, and there are no surer guarantees of equality among men than poverty and misfortune."

—Alexis de Tocqueville

The early settlers to America came mainly from northern and western Europe and predominantly from England, Ireland, France, Germany, Scandinavia, and Holland. By the beginning of the Gilded Age, these nationalities had become established as Americans. But the seemingly insatiable need of labor encouraged a new wave of immigrants from other countries, and this concerned some Americans who were worried that this influx of different nationalities might fundamentally change the nature of their society.

The new immigrants who arrived in huge numbers during the Gilded Age came from two distinct sources. First, there were southern and eastern Europeans including Italians, Greeks, Poles, Russians, and Slovaks amongst others. These settlers arriving on the east coast were attracted by higher wages and plentiful work opportunities. Many were illiterate, even in their native tongue, and few spoke or understood English. Few had experience of democratic government and most were Roman Catholics (the United States was predominantly Protestant until this time). Many of these immigrants lived in tight-knit ethnic groups which created enclaves like Little Italy and Greektown in New York City.

The other main source of immigrants was Asia, and particularly China. Chinese immigrants began arriving on the west coast of America in the 1830s, but only in relatively small numbers, and many were so-called "birds of passage," single male immigrants who came to the U.S. for a time to work and then returned to their own country with their savings. Like many immigrants, the Chinese tended to settle in existing ethnic areas, and many American cities in the west had their own Chinatown. The California Gold Rush combined with famine, poverty, and political upheaval in China in the 1840s attracted larger numbers of Chinese immigrants to America. From 1861 to 1890, almost quarter of a million Chinese immigrants arrived in the United States; they worked in a range of menial, low-paid jobs including cleaning, laundry, and as laborers on farms and railroad construction crews. They were popular as employees because they were hard working, willing to work for low wages, and virtually none were members of a union.

Unlike European settlers, Chinese immigrants did not generally assimilate into American society. Partly, this was because their appearance made them look so different—the wearing of the queue (a hairstyle that featured long, braided hair) for example seemed odd, unhygienic, and unmanly to many Americans. For Chinese immigrants, the queue was very necessary—any Chinese person in China without a queue was liable to execution, and many of the Chinese working in the U.S. planned to return to their homeland. This distinctive physical difference combined with the tendency of Chinese immigrants to mingle only with other Chinese made them seem odd and suspicious to many Americans.

While work was plentiful, no-one seemed to particularly mind the presence of the Chinese, but when recession struck in 1873, the Chinese found themselves competing with Americans and immigrants from Europe for jobs. Suddenly, their differences made the Chinese a target for resentment in

America. Tales began to spread of the use of opium by Chinese communities as well as prostitution and gambling within Chinatowns. There was a measure of truth in these stories, but in reality the Chinese simply became an easily identifiable target for racial discrimination. In the 1870s, legislation was passed in the State of California that limited the number of Chinese immigrants who would be allowed to enter the country. In 1882, Congress passed the Chinese Exclusion Act which prohibited the immigration of Chinese people to the U.S. for ten years. The act was later extended for a further ten years and then indefinitely, prohibiting Chinese immigration to the United States for half a century.

The sheer number of immigrants arriving in America during the Gilded Age was huge. For example, in the period 1877-1890, over six million immigrants arrived in the United States. This represented a ten percent increase in the total population and, inevitably, it did change the ethnic mix of many cities. By the end of the century, 15 percent of the population had not been born in the U.S., and in parts of cities such as New York and Chicago, up to 80 percent of residents had not been born in America. The existence of poor ghettos where people spoke their own languages increased suspicion of immigrants amongst existing Americans, and groups like the Immigration Restriction League, founded in 1894, claimed that the issue was "a race question, pure and simple. . . . It is fundamentally a question as to what kind of babies shall be born; it is a question as to what races shall dominate in this country."

This concern about immigrants fundamentally changing America became heated during the Gilded Age and led directly in the twentieth century to legislation limiting immigration to the country. Some of the most vociferous opponents to uncontrolled immigration were those who objected on religious grounds.

Chapter Eight

Religion

"It is a time when one's spirit is subdued and sad, one knows not why; when the past seems a storm-swept desolation, life a vanity and a burden, and the future but a way to death."

—Mark Twain, *The Gilded Age*

Urbanization and mechanization in the workplace encouraged vast numbers of people to move from rural to urban areas during the Gilded Age. The massive influx of immigrants during the same period added to feelings of alienation and a loss of social identity. Traditional models of relationships and social interaction were changed radically as were attitudes towards religion.

Prior to the Gilded Age, the majority of Americans were Protestant. While the Episcopal Church was the largest, there were also large Baptist, Methodist, and Presbyterian churches in various parts of the country. Smaller numbers of Roman Catholics from Ireland and Germany had their own churches, mainly on the east coast. Immigration increased the proportion of Roman Catholics and introduced many Jews fleeing persecution in Europe. These changes, combined with the emergence of new scientific knowledge which appeared to challenge traditional Christian values (Darwin's *The Origin of Species* was published in 1858) led many people to question existing religious practice which, in turn, led to the emergence of a number of new views of theology and to the creation of completely new religious movements during this period.

In the United States, as in most Christian countries at this time, there was a battle between two diametrically opposed viewpoints: Liberal Theology and Fundamentalism. Liberal Theology (often associated in the U.S. with Unitarianism) focused less on the miraculous elements of religion and more on the human factor. This viewpoint sought ways of assimilating new scientific knowledge within existing Christian theology. Discussing evolution, for example, Washington Gladden, Pastor of the First Congregational Church in Columbus, Ohio said: "This modern science which has been supposed by some persons to have banished God from the universe, has not, then banished order from the universe; it has given us revelations of the order and system which pervades the whole far more impressive than our fathers ever saw. It has not banished purpose from the universe. Why, then, should we cease to believe in an intelligent Creator?"

Fundamentalists were directly opposed to this view, resisted change, and wanted a return to basic theological values. Fundamentalists tended either to ignore new scientific thinking or to try to include it in existing religious views—for example, fundamentalists claimed that dinosaur fossils were not remnants of ancient creatures but were created as fossils when God created the Earth in the relatively recent past.

This dichotomy in religious thinking led to the creation of some completely new religious movements during the Gilded Age. For example, the group that later became known as Jehovah's Witnesses was founded in the 1870s by Charles Taze Russell, a minister from Pittsburgh, Pennsylvania, who believed in a return to a more pure and ancient form of Christianity through study of the bible. In 1879, a woman named Mary Baker Eddy and a group of her followers founded a new church in Boston, the Church of Christ, Scientist. This church postulated the view that what we consider the material world is actually an illusion and that things like physical illness should be treated by prayer. Christianity was also being challenged by new groups such as Spiritualist organizations which were not directly religious but believed in communication with the spirits of the dead.

During the Gilded Age, membership of religious groups in America increased, in contrast to Europe where the church was becoming less important. Materialism was on the rise and access to the products of industry were available to more Americans than ever before, but this seemed to increase rather than decrease interest in spirituality. However, religion became more and more fragmented in the same period. White Protestants still tended to see themselves as the archetypical Americans, but they were being challenged by religious practices which were associated with immigrants and by completely new religious which either espoused advances in science or completely rejected them. Radical nationalist and racist groups such as the Know-Nothing Party and the Ku Klux Klan did their best to identify the Protestant religion with being American. Over time and generally after the Gilded Age had ended, white Catholics and Jewish immigrants gradually also became accepted as being American, but there remained deep suspicion of religions associated with Native Americans, African Americans, and Asian Americans.

Like many aspects of the Gilded Age, religion tended to be a divisive rather than a cohesive force during this era.

Chapter Nine

Invention and Innovation

"We will make electricity so cheap that only the rich will burn candles."

—Thomas Edison

Combined with the social and political changes of the Gilded Age, this period also saw profound change due to technical innovation. No single invention of this period had a greater impact on day-to-day life than the creation of the first practical incandescent light bulb produced by Thomas Edison in 1878. Thomas Edison didn't invent the electric light bulb—Humphry Davy produced the first electric arc lamp in 1802, which didn't last long as it was simply too bright. Thomas Edison was a prolific inventor (he registered more than one thousand original patents in the United States during his lifetime), and he used the proceeds from the sale of the patent for his quadruplex telegraph to build a laboratory in Menlo Park, New Jersey. There, he started research on, amongst other things, electric lighting.

At that time, most American cities and many homes and businesses were lit by dangerous, unreliable, and not particularly bright gas lamps. In 1878, with the assistance of financier J. P. Morgan, Edison formed the Edison Electric Light Company in New York City. By 1880, he had refined the design of his light bulb to produce a version that would last for 1,200 hours, a great improvement on previous designs. In the same year he formed the Edison Illuminating Company to market his patented version of an electricity distribution system. The very first power station in the

United States was opened on Pearl Street in lower Manhattan, New York City and provided 59 customers with 110 volts direct current (DC) electrical supply.

People were stunned by electric lighting. It was not only bright and steady, but it also cost less and was safer than gas lighting. Electric lighting, especially in streets and public spaces, spread across America with unbelievable speed. At the World's Fair of 1893 in Chicago, over 100,00 electric bulbs were installed, and the exhibition became known as the City of Light. It was, claimed one breathless visitor, "like getting a sudden vision of Heaven." The increasing availability of reliable electricity supply in American cities also made possible the use of a whole host of other electrical appliances such as telephones, wireless receivers, and electric refrigerators.

The telephone was another revolutionary new device which emerged during the Gilded Age. In 1875, Alexander Graham Bell applied for a patent for an electric telegraph. In 1876, he made the first voice telephone call, and just two years later the first commercial telephone exchange in America was opened at New Haven in Connecticut. By 1900, there were more than 600,000 telephones in the United States and people were already wondering how they had ever managed without this wonderful new invention.

Other inventions during this period were less obvious but had a profound impact. The expanded railroad system was combined with the invention of the refrigerated railroad car around 1870 to allow for the first time the transport of meat and other perishable goods far from the areas where they were produced. The almost complete shift from sailing ships to steam-powered vessels during the period of the Gilded Age made transport by sea faster, cheaper, and more predictable.

When it came to cars, the internal combustion engine also began to replace the steam engine during the Gilded

Age. In 1885, Karl Benz offered the first production motorcar with a gasoline-powered engine for sale in Germany. In 1893, the Duryea Motor Wagon Company became the first American automobile manufacturer, and by the end of the Gilded Age, Henry Ford had started building automobiles as had the Autocar Company and the Olds Motor Vehicle Company (later to become Oldsmobile).

The streets of many American cities, which had started the Gilded Age filled with horse-drawn carts and carriages, were by 1900 also thronged with steam and gasoline-powered vehicles as well as electric trams and trains. Under those streets, electrically-powered subway trains provided yet another means of rapid transit in some cities. The buildings which framed the streets had also changed. In 1885, a ten-story steel-framed office building, the Home Insurance Building, was erected in Chicago and caused a sensation. Here was a building which would help avoid the problems caused by a lack of available building land and yet still looked modern and elegant. In Chicago and New York City, many more steel-framed multi-story buildings were erected in the second half of the Gilded Age, and the term "skyscraper" became commonly used to describe these imposingly tall structures. Many of these new buildings were designed from the outset to include electric lighting and telephones. In just 30 years, from 1870 to 1900, most major U.S. cities changed beyond recognition.

There was one invention under development during the Gilded Age which was not widely known and which most people would have regarded as being within the realm of science fiction. In a shed just outside Dayton, Ohio, two brothers, Orville and Wilbur Wright, had produced one of the very first viable and controllable flying machines and had secretly tested it before the Gilded Age ended. Their machine was a glider, and it would be three years later, in 1903, that they would combine this machine with a small internal combustion engine to become the first men to take to the air in a powered flying machine. America and the world would never be quite the same again.

Conclusion

The Gilded Age was a period of profound and extremely rapid change in the United States of America. After the Civil War, there were strenuous attempts to unite the north and the south, and migration populated the west with eager settlers. Major urban centers grew and attracted the majority of the U.S. population. New technologies like electricity, the telephone, and the internal combustion engine changed life for a great many Americans. Immigrants from different parts of the world changed the very face of U.S. society, and people began looking at new religions and new forms of spirituality.

This was a period of enormous contrast. The west was still wild during the early part of this period while the east became developed as a series of modern, industrial cities. An almost complete lack of regulation allowed a small number of ambitious entrepreneurs to build monopolies based on emerging technologies, and in the process these men became fantastically wealthy. The vast majority of people lived in very different circumstances, crowded into unsanitary housing and working long hours for little pay, generally unprotected by government or unions. The contrast between the beginning and end of this era is also very striking. In just 30 years, electric power and light, telephones, skyscrapers, and gasoline-powered vehicles became commonplace in many American cities.

America entered the Gilded Age ravaged by war and as a mainly agrarian society. It ended this era as one of the foremost industrial powers in the world.

Printed in Dunstable, United Kingdom

65231557R00030